The Christmas Ukulele Songbook

Top - Requested Christmas Songs
26 Best Songs

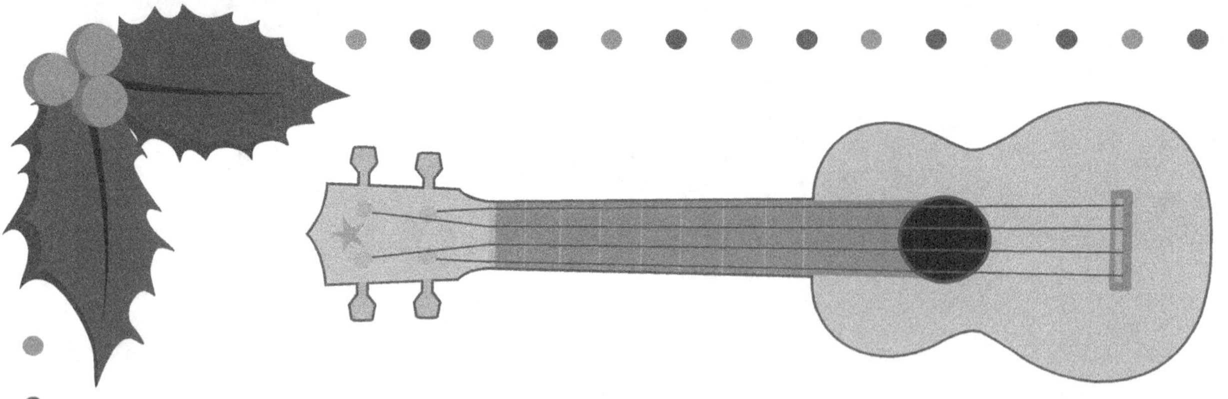

Christmas Ukulele Contents

<u>Away In A Manger</u>—Traditional

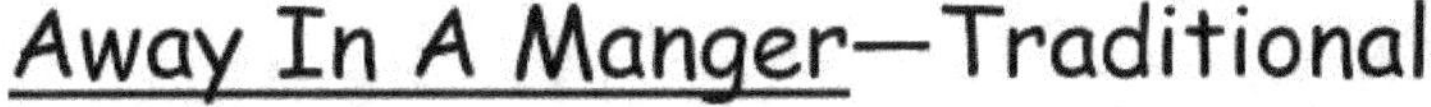

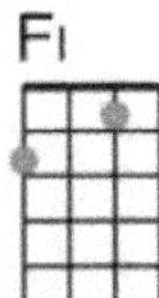 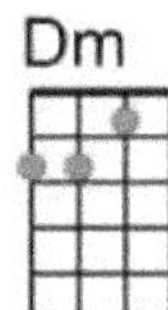 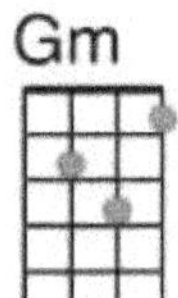 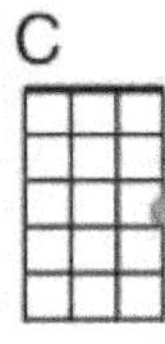 

(C7) A- (F) -way in a manger,
No (F) crib for (Dm) a (Gm) bed,
The (C7) little lord (F) Jesus (Dm) laid (G7) down his sweet (C) head.
(C7) The (F) stars in the bright sky,
Looked down where (Dm) he (Gm) lay,
The (C7) little lord (F) Jesus, (Dm) a-(Gm)-sleep on (C7) the (F) hay.

(C7) The (F) cattle are lowing,
The baby (Dm) a-(Gm)-wakes,
The (C7) little lord (F) Jesus (Dm) no (G7) crying he (C) makes.
(C7) I (F) love thee lord Jesus,
Look (F) down from (Dm) the (Gm) sky
And (C7) stay by my (F) bedside (Dm) till (Gm) morning (C7) is (F) nigh.

(C7) Be (F) near me lord Jesus,
I ask thee (Dm) to (Gm) stay,
Close (C7) by me for (F) ever (Dm) and (G7) love me I (C) pray.
(C7) Bless (F) all the dear children,
In (F) thy ten-(Dm)-der (Gm) care,
And (C7) fit us for (F) heaven (Dm) to (Gm) live with (C7) thee
(F) there.

<u>Blue Christmas</u> —Hayes&Johnson

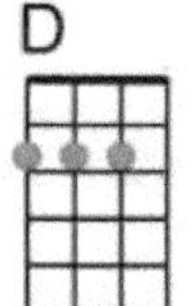 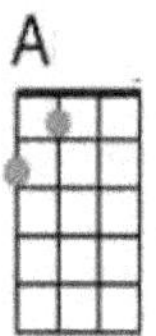 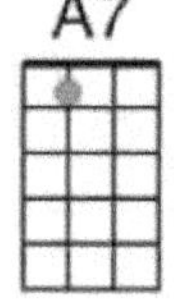 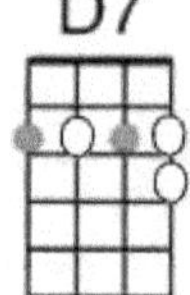 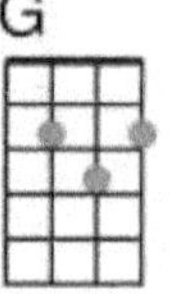 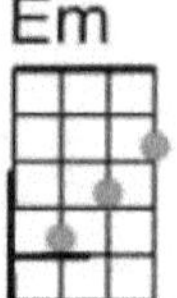 

I'll have a (D) blue Christmas (A) without you,
I'll be so blue just (A7) thinking (D) about you. (D7)
Decor-(D)-ations of (D7) red on a (G) green Christmas tree, (Em)
(E7) Won't be the same dear, if (A) you're not here with (A7) me.

And when those (D) blue snowflakes start (A) fallin',
That's when those blue (A7) memories start (D) callin' (D7)
You'll be (D) doin' (D7) all right with your (G) Christmas of (Em) white
But (A) I'll have a blue, blue, blue, blue (D) Christmas. (A)

(D) Mmm mm mm mm (D) Mmm mm mm mm
(A) Mmm mm mm mm (A) Mmm mm mm mm
(A7) Mmm mm mm mm (A7) Mmm mm mm mm
(D) Mmm mm mm mm mm mm

You'll be (D) doin' (D7) all right with your (G) Christmas of (Em) white
But (A) I'll have a blue, blue, blue, blue (D) Christmas. (A)

Deck The Halls—Traditional

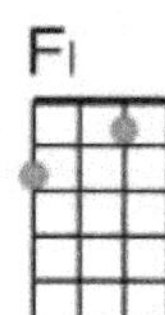

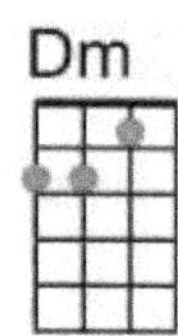
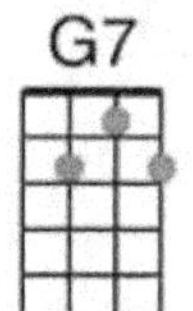
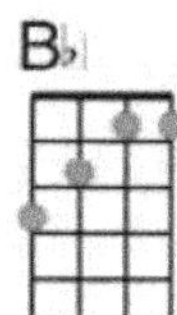

(F) Deck the halls with boughs of holly
(C7) Fa la la la (F) laa, la (C7) la la (F) laa
(F) Tis the season to be jolly,
(C7) Fa la la la (F) laa, la (C7) la la (F) laa
(C7) Don we now our (F) gay (C) apparel
(F) Fa la laa (Dm) la la (G7) la la (C) la
(F) Troll the ancient Yuletide carol
(Bb) Fa la la la (F) la, la la (C7) la (F) la.

(F) See the blazing Yule before us,
(C7) Fa la la la (F) laa, la (C7) la la (F) laa
(F) Strike the harp and join the chorus,
(C7) Fa la la la (F) laa, la (C7) la la (F) laa
(C7) Follow me in (F) merry (C) measure
(F) Fa la laa (Dm) la la (G7) la la (C) la
(F) While I tell of Yuletide treasure,
(Bb) Fa la la la (F) la, la la (C7) la (F) la.

(F) Fast away the old year passes,
(C7) Fa la la la (F) laa, la (C7) la la (F) laa
(F) Hail the new, ye lads and lasses
(C7) Fa la la la (F) laa, la (C7) la la (F) laa
(C7) Sing we joyous (F) all (C) together,
(F) Fa la laa (Dm) la la (G7) la la (C) la
(F) Heedless of the wind and weather,
(Bb) Fa la la la (F) la, la la (C7) la (F) la.

<u>Do They know It's Christmas?</u>—Band Aid

(C) It's Christmas (F) time, there's no need to be (C) afraid.
At Christmas (F) time, we let in light and we (C) banish shade.
And in our (Dm) world of (G) plenty we can (C) spread a smile of (F) joy,
Throw your (Dm) arms around the (G) world at Christmas (C) time.

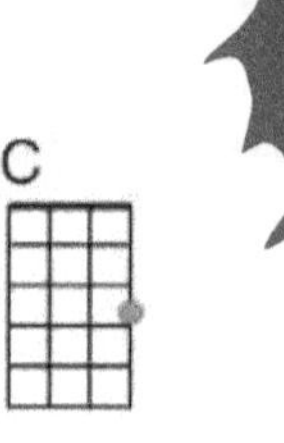
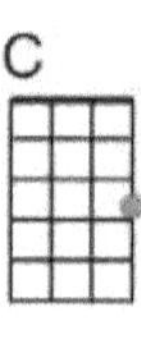

But say a (F) prayer; (G) pray for the (C) other ones,
At Christmas (F) time, it's (G) hard, but when you're (C) having fun
There's a (F) world outside your (G) window,
And it's a (C) world of dread and (F) fear,
Where the (Dm) only water (G) flowing is
The (C) bitter sting of (F) tears.
And the (Dm) Christmas bells that (G) ring there
Are the (C) clanging chimes of (F) doom.
Well, (Dm) tonight thank God it's (G) them, instead of (C) you.

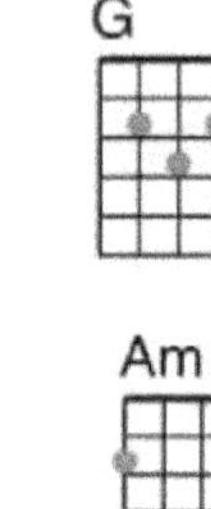
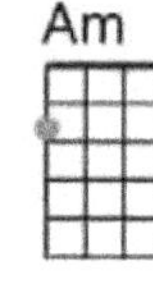

And there (F) won't be snow in (G) Africa this (C) Christmas time.
The (F) greatest gift they'll (G) get this year is (C) life. (C7)
Where (F) nothing ever (G) grows, no (C) rain nor rivers (F) flow,
(Dm) Do they know it's (G) Christmas time at (C) all? (F)(C)

(Am) Here's to you; (G) Raise a glass for everyone.
(Am) Here's to them; (G) Underneath that burning sun
(Dm) Do they know it's (G) Christmas time at (C) all? (F)(C)

(C)(F)(C)(F)(C)(Dm)(G) x2
(C) Feed the (F) world! (C)   (F)(C)Dm)(G)
(C) Feed the (F) world! (C)   (F)(C)Dm)(G)

(C) Feed the (F) world! (C)
(F) Let them (C) know it's (Dm) Christmas time (G) again!
(C) Feed the (F) world! (C)
(F) Let them (C) know it's (Dm) Christmas time (G) again!
(C) Feed the (F) world! (C)
(F) Let them (C) know it's (Dm) Christmas time (G) again!

Frosty The Snowman—Nelson&Rollins

(C)   Frosty the Snowman was a (F) jolly, (G7) happy (C) soul,
With a (F) corncob pipe and a (C) button nose
And two (G7) eyes made out of (C) coal.
Frosty the Snowman is a (F) fairy (G7) tale they (C) say,
He was (F) made of snow but the (C) children know
How he (Dm) came to (G7) life one (C7) day.

There (F) must have been some (Em) magic in that
(Dm) Old silk (G7) hat they (C) found,
For (G) when they placed it on his head,
He (Am) began to (D7) dance (G) around.

(C) Frosty the Snowman was (F) alive as (G7) he could (C) be,
And the (F) children say he could (C) dance and play
Just the (Dm) same as (G7) you and (C) me.

Frosty the Snowman knew the (F) sun was (G7) hot that (C) day,
So he said (F) "Let's run, we'll have (C) lots of fun
Now (G7) before I melt (C) away.".
Down in the village with a (F) broomstick (G7) in his (C) hand,
Running (F) here and there all (C) around the square
Saying (Dm) "Catch me (G7) if you (C7) can!"

He (F) lead them down the (Em) streets of town
Right (Dm) to a (G7) traffic (C) cop,
And he (G) only paused one moment when
He (Am) heard them (D7) holler (G) " Stop!"

For (C) Frosty the Snowman had to (F) hurry (G7) on his (C) way,

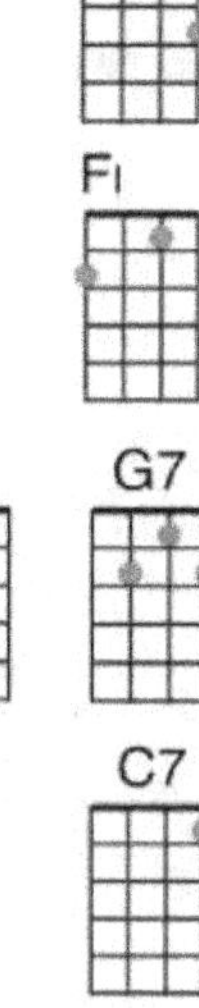

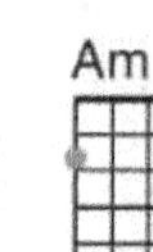

<u>Happy Xmas (War Is Over)</u> —Lennon & Ono

So this is (G) Christmas, and what have you (Am) done?
Another year (D) over, a new one just (G) begun.
And (G7) so this is (C) Christmas, I hope you have (Dm) fun
The near and the (G) dear ones, the old and the (C) young.

A (C7) merry, merry (F) Christmas, and a happy New (G) Year
Let's hope it's a (Dm) good one (F) without any (C) fears. (D)

And (D7) so this is (G) Christmas, (War is over)
For weak and for (Am) strong. (If you want it)
The rich and the (D) poor ones (War is over)
The road is so (G) long. (Now)
And (G7) so happy (C) Christmas, (War is over)
For black and for (Dm) white. (If you want it)
For yellow and (G) red ones, (War is over)
Let's stop all the (C) fights. (Now)

A (C7) merry, merry (F) Christmas, and a happy New (G) Year
Let's hope it's a (Dm) good one (F) without any (C) fears. (D)

And (D7) so this is (G) Christmas, (War is over)
And what have we (Am) done? (If you want it)
Another year (D) over, (War is over)
A new one just (G) begun. (Now)
And (G7) so this is (C) Christmas, (War is over)
We hope you have (Dm) fun (If you want it)
The near and the (G) dear ones, (War is over)
The old and the (C) young. (Now)

A (C7) merry, merry (F) Christmas, and a happy New (G) Year
Let's hope it's a (Dm) good one (F) without any (C) fears. (D)

(G) War is over, (Am) if you want it. (D) War is over, (G) now...
(G) War is over, (Am) if you want it. (D) War is over, (G) now...

G
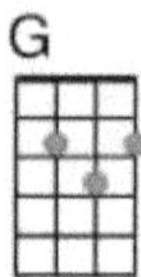

Am
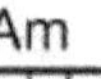

D
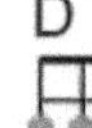

G7

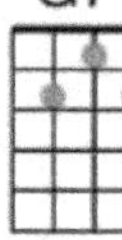

Dm

C
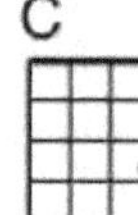

D7
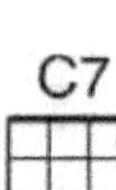

C7
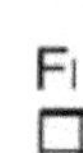

F

<u>Have Yourself A Merry Little Christmas—</u>
Martin & Blane

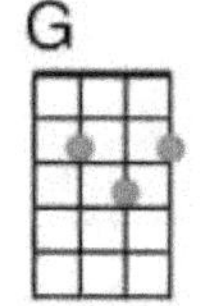 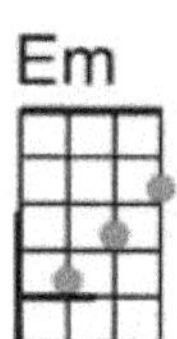  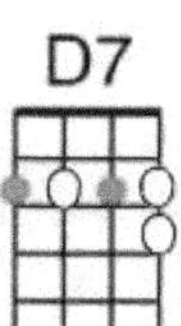 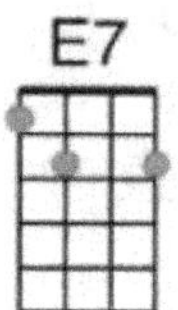 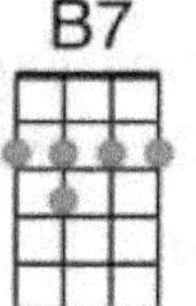  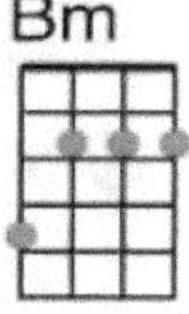 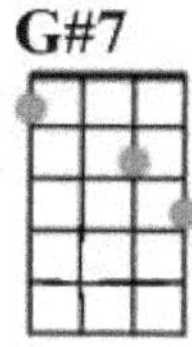

(G) Have your-(Em) -self a (Am) merry little (D7) Christmas
(G) Let your (Em) heart be (Am) light, (D7)
(G) From now (Em) on your
(Am) Troubles will be (D7) out of (E7) sight.   -(A7) (D7)

(G) Have your-(Em)-self a (Am) merry little (D7) Christmas
(G) Make the (Em) yuletide (Am) gay, (D7)
(G) From now (Em) on your
(Am) Troubles will be (B7) miles (Em) away.   -(G)

(Em) Once again as in (D) olden days
Happy (Am) golden days (D7) of (G#7) yore.
(Em) Faithful friends who are (Bm) dear to us
Shall be (D) near to us once (Am) more. (D7)

(G) Someday (Em) soon we (Am) all will be (D) together,
(G) If the (Em) fates (Am) allow, (D7)
(G) Until (Em) then we'll (Am) have to muddle (D7) through (Em) some-
how.
So (C) have yourself a (Am) merry little (D7) Christmas (G) now.

<u>I Wish It Could Be Christmas Every Day</u> — Roy Wood

Oh when the (C) snowman brings the snow
Oh well he (F) just might like to know
He's put a (C) great big smile up- (Am) -on somebody's face. (Dm)(G)
If you (C) jump into your bed,
Quickly (F) cover up your (D7) head,
Don't you (C) lock your door, you know that
(G) Sweet Santa Claus is on his (Bb) way. (C)

(CHORUS)
Oh (Bb) well I (D) wish it could be Christmas every (G) day.
When the (A7) kids start singing and the band begins to play. (D)(A7)
(D) Oh I wish it could be Christmas every (G) day
So let the bells ring (A7) out for (G) Christmas! (D)

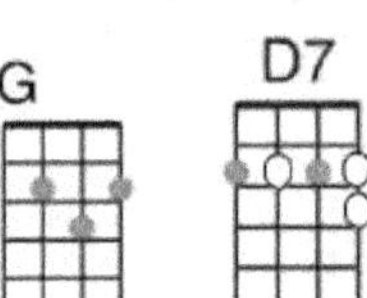

When we're (C) skating in the park,
If the (F) storm cloud paints it dark
Then your (C) rosy cheeks gonna (Am) light my merry way. (Dm)(G)
Now the (C) 'frosticals' appeared
And they've (F) frozen up my (D7) beard,
So we'll (C) lie by the fire till the
(G) Sleep simply melts them all (C) away. (D)

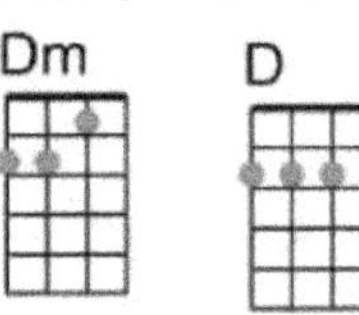

CHORUS

When the (C) snowman brings the snow
Oh well he (F) just might like to know
He's put a (C) great big smile up- (Am) -on somebody's face. (Dm)(G)
So if (C) santa brings the sleigh
All (F) along that Milky (D7) Way,
I'll sign my (C) name on the rooftop in the
(G) Snow then he may decide to (Bb) stay. (C)

CHROUS plus-
Why don't you (G) give your (A) love for (G) Christmas? (D)
When the (D) snowman brings the snow... (*repeat to fade*)

I'm Dreaming of a White Christmas—Traditional

(G) I'm dreaming of a (Am) white (D) Christmas,
(C) Just like the (D) ones I used to (G) know,
Where the tree tops (G7) glisten and (C) children (Cm) listen,
To (G) hear (Em) sleigh bells in the (Am) snow. (D)

(G) I'm dreaming of a (Am) white (D) Christmas,
(C) With every (D) Christmas card I (G) write,
May your days be (G7) merry and (C) bright (Cm)
And may (G) all your (Am) Christmasses (D) be (G) white. (D)

(G) I'm dreaming of a (Am) white (D) Christmas,
(C) Just like the (D) ones I used to (G) know,
Where the tree tops (G7) glisten and (C) children (Cm) listen,
To (G) hear (Em) sleigh bells in the (Am) snow. (D)

(G) I'm dreaming of a (Am) white (D) Christmas,
(C) With every (D) Christmas card I (G) write,
May your days be (G7) merry and (C) bright (Cm)
And may (G) all your (Am) Christmasses (D) be (G) white.

<u>Jingle Bells</u>—J.S. Pierpont

 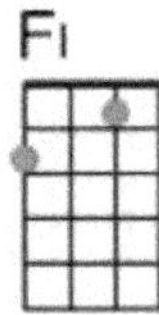  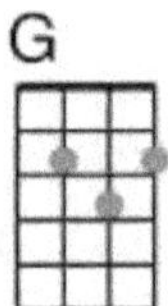 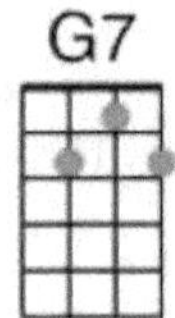

(C) Jingle bells, jingle bells, jingle all the way,
(F) Oh, what fun it (C) is to ride
In a (D) one-horse open (G) sleigh, (G7) hey!
(C) Jingle bells, jingle bells, jingle all the way,
(F) Oh, what fun it (C) is to ride
In a (G) one-horse (G7) open (C) sleigh.

We're (C) Dashing through the snow
In a one-horse open (F) sleigh,
Across the fields we (G) go,
(G7) Laughing all the (C) way.
Bells on bobtails ring,
Making spirits (F) bright,
What fun it is to (G) ride and sing a (G7) sleighing
song (C) tonight.

(C) Jingle bells, jingle bells, jingle all the way,
(F) Oh, what fun it (C) is to ride
In a (D) one-horse open (G) sleigh, (G7) hey!
(C) Jingle bells, jingle bells, jingle all the way,
(F) Oh, what fun it (C) is to ride
In a (G) one-horse (G7) open (C) sleigh.

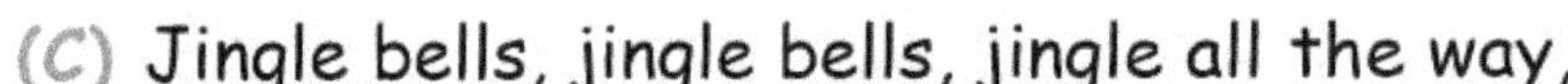

<u>Last Christmas</u> —George Michael

(C) Last Christmas I gave you my heart,
But the (Am) very next day you gave it away,
(Dm) This year to save me from tears,
I'll (G) give it to someone special.
(C) Last Christmas I gave you my heart,
But the (Am) very next day you gave it away,
(Dm) This year to save me from tears,
I'll (G) give it to someone special.

(C) Once bitten and twice shy,
(Am) I keep my distance, but you still catch my eye,
(F) Tell me baby, do you recognize me?
(G) Well, it's been a year, it doesn't surprise me.
(C) (*Happy Christmas*) I wrapped it up and sent it,
(Am) With a note saying, "I love you" , I meant it,
(Dm) Now I know what a fool I've been,
But if you (G) kissed me now, I know you'd fool me again.

CHORUS

(C) A crowded room, friends with tired eyes,
(Am) I'm hiding from you, and your soul of ice,
(F) My god, I thought you were someone to rely on,
(G) Me? I guess I was a shoulder to cry on.
(C) A face on a lover with a fire in his heart,
(Am) A man under cover but you tore me apart,
(Dm) Oh, oh
Now I've (G) found a real love you'll never fool me again.

CHORUS

Let It Snow—
Martina McBride

Oh, the (D) weather (A) outside is (D) frightful,
But the (A) fire is so (A7) delightful,
And (Em) since we've no place to go,
Let it (A) snow, let it (A7) snow, let it (D) snow.

Oh, it (D) doesn't show (A) signs of (D) stopping,
And I've (A) brought some corn for (A7) popping,
The (Em) lights are turned way down low,
Let it (A) snow, let it (A7) snow, let it (D) snow.

When we (A) finally kiss good night,
How I (E7) hate going out in the (A) storm.
But if you really hold me tight,
(D7) All the way (E7) home I'll be (A) warm.   (A7)

Oh, the (D) fire is (A) slowly (D) dying,
And my (A) dear we're still (A7) good-bye-ing ,
But as (Em) long as you love me so,
Let it (A) snow, let it (A7) snow, let it (D) snow.

When we (A) finally kiss good night,
How I (E7) hate going out in the (A) storm.
But if you really hold me tight,
(D7) All the way (E7) home I'll be (A) warm.   (A7)

Oh, the (D) fire is (A) slowly (D) dying,
And my (A) dear we're still (A7) good-bye-ing ,
But as (Em) long as you love me so,
Let it (A) snow, let it (A7) snow, let it (D) snow.
Let it (A) snow, let it (A7) snow, and (D) snow.

D

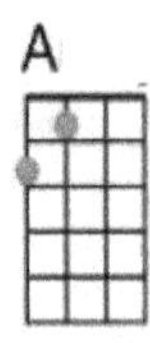

A

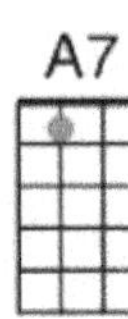

A7

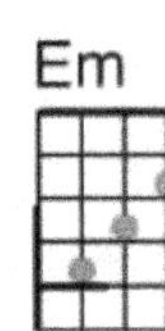

Em

E7

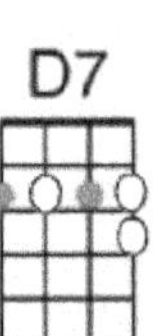

D7

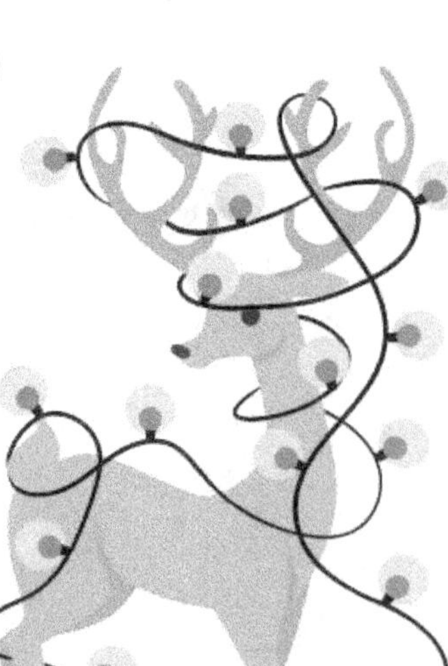

<u>Mary's Boy Child—Boney M</u>

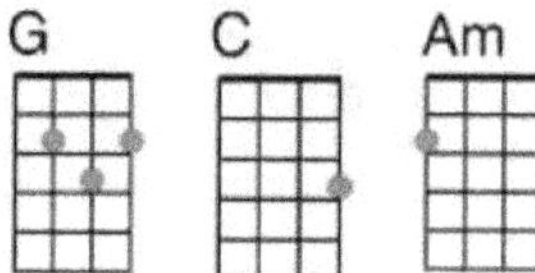

(G) Long time ago in (C) Bethlehem (Am) so the (D) Holy Bible (G) say,
Mary's boy-child, (C) Jesus (Am) Christ was (G) born on (D) Christmas (G) Day.

CHORUS
Hark now! (C) Hear the (D) angels (G) sing,
A (Em) king was (Am) born (D) today,
And (G) man will live (C) forever (Am) more
(G) Because of (D) Christmas (G) day.

(G) While shepherds what their (C) flocks by (Am) night they see a (D) bright new
shining (G) star,
They hear a choir (C) sing a (Am) song the music (G) seemed to (D) come from (G)
afar.
(Chorus)

(G) Now Joseph and his (C) wife (Am) Mary came to (D) Bethlehem (G) that night,
They found no place to (C) bear the (Am) child not a (G) single (D) room was in (G)
sight.
(Chorus)

(G) By and by they found a (C) little (Am) nook in a (D) stable all (G) forlorn
And in a manger (C) cold and (Am) dark, Mary's (G) little (D) boy was (G) born.

Chorus +

Trumpets (C) sound and (D) angels (G) sing, (Em) listen to (Am) what they (D) say,
That (G) man will live (C) forever (Am) more (G) because of (D) Christmas (G) day.

(G) Oh my lord, you sent your son to save us
Oh my lord, your very self you gave us
(D) Oh my lord, that sin will not enslave us,
(G) And love may reign once more.
Oh my lord, when in the crib they found him
Oh my lord, a golden halo crowned him
(D) Oh my lord, they gathered all around him
(G) To see him and adore... (*His light is shining on us all*)
Oh my lord, (*So praise the lord!*) they had begun to doubt you.
Oh my lord, (*He is the truth forever*) what did they know about you?
(D) Oh my lord, (*So praise the lord*) but they were lost without you
(G)They needed you so bad.
(*His light is* (D) *shining on us* (G) *all*)

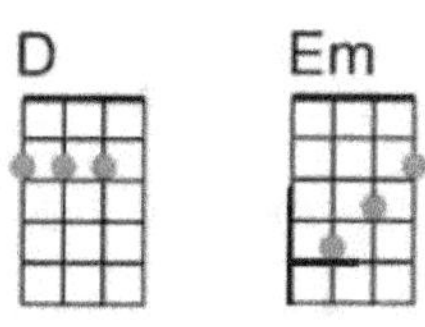

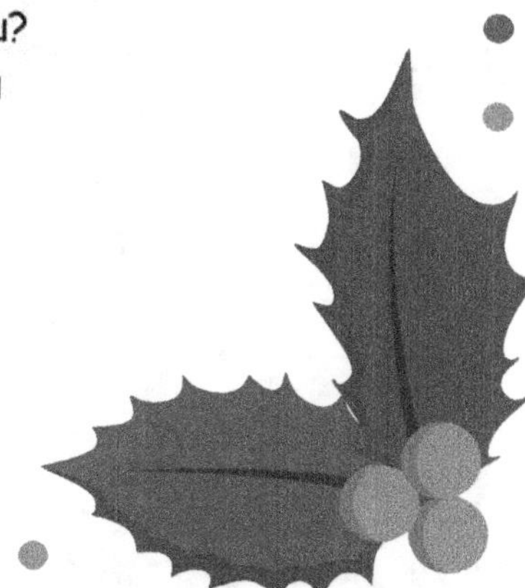

<u>Merry Christmas Everyone</u>—Shakin Stevens

Snow is (G) falling (D) all a-(Em)-round me (C)
Children (G) playing (C), having (G) fun.
It's the season of love and under- (Em) -standing, (C)
Merry (G) Christmas (D) everyone! (G)

Time for (G) parties and celeb-(Em)-ration (C)
People (G) dancing (C) all night (G) long
Time for presents and exchanging (Em) kisses (C)
Time for (G) singing (D) Christmas (G) songs.

(Em) We're gonna (C) have a (G) party (D) tonight, (Em)
I'm gonna (C) find that girl,
(G) Underneath the misteltoe, and (D) kiss by candlelight .

Room is (G) swaying, (D) records (Em) playing (C)
All the (G) old songs, (C) love to (G) hear.
Oh I wish that every day was (Em) Christmas (C)
What a (G) nice way to (D) spend a (G) year.

(Em) We're gonna (C) have a (G) party (D) tonight, (Em)
I'm gonna (C) find that girl,
(G) Underneath the misteltoe, and (D) kiss by candlelight

Room is (G) swaying, (D) records (Em) playing (C)
All the (G) old songs, (C) love to (G) hear.
Oh I wish that every day was (Em) Christmas (C)
What a (G) nice way to (D) spend a (G) year.

Ooo, snow is (G) falling (D) all a-(Em)-round me (C)
Children (G) playing (C), having (G) fun.
It's the season love and under- (Em) -standing, (C)
Merry (G) Christmas (D) everyone! (G) (C)
Merry (G) Christmas (D) everyone! (G) (C)
Oh, merry (G) Christmas (D) everyone! (G)

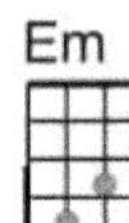

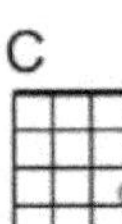

Merry Xmas Everybody—Slade

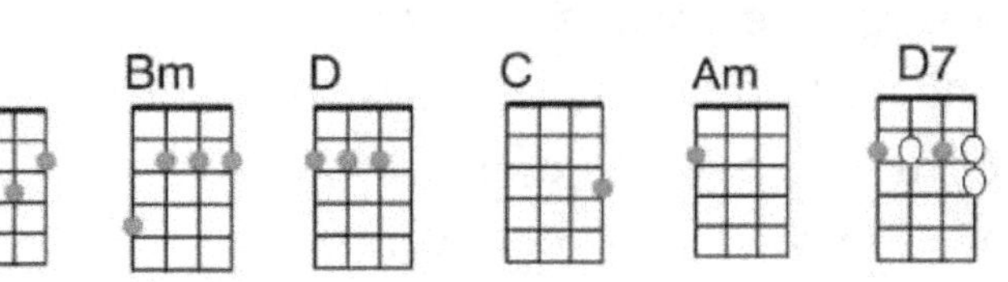

Are you (G) hanging up the (Bm) stocking on the (D) wall ?
It's the (G) time that every (Bm) Santa has a (D) ball ?
Does he (C) ride a red-nosed (G) reindeer ?
Does a (C) ton upon his (G) sleigh ?
Do the (Am) fairies keep him sober for a (D) day ? (D7)

CHORUS
So here it (G) is, 'Merry (Bm) Christmas',
Every- (Bb) -body's having (D) fun,
(G) Look to the (Bm) future now, it's (Bb) only just begun (D) .

Are you (G) waiting for the (Bm) family to (D) arrive ?
Are you (G) sure you've got the (Bm) room to spare (D) inside ?
Does your (C) granny always (G) tell ya'
That the (C) old songs are the (G) best?
Then she's (Am) up and rock and rollin' with the (D) rest. (D7)

CHORUS

(Dm) What will your daddy (Bb) do when he sees your
(Dm) Mamma kissin' (Bb) Santa Claus? (C) Ah-aaa– (D) aa

Are you (G) hanging up the (Bm) stocking on the (D) wall ?
Are you (G) hoping that the (Bm) snow will start to (D) fall ?
Do you (C) ride on down the (G) hillside
In a (C) buggy you have (G) made ?
When you (Am) land upon your head then you bin' (D) slayed! (D7)

CHORUS (x4)

Mistletoe & Wine—Cliff Richard

The (G) child is a king, the carollers sing,
The (Em) old has passed, there's a (D) new beginning.
(C) Dreams of Santa, (G) dreams of snow,
(A) Fingers numb, (D) faces (D7) aglow, it's…

(G) Christmas time, mistletoe and wine,
Children singing (D) Christian rhyme.
With logs on the fire and gifts on the tree,
A time to (D7) rejoice in the (G) good that we see.

A (G) time for living, a time for believing
A (Em) time for trusting (D) not deceiving
(C) Love and laughter and (G) joy ever after,
(A) Ours for the taking, just (D) follow the (D7) master, it's…

(G) Christmas time, mistletoe and wine,
Children singing (D) Christian rhyme.
With logs on the fire and gifts on the tree,
A time to (D7) rejoice in the (G) good that we see.

It's a (G) time for giving, a time for getting,
A (Em) time for forgiving (D) and for forgetting
(C) Christmas is love (G) Christmas is peace
(A) A time for hating and (D) fighting to (D7) cease. (Hold for 4 beats)

(G) Christmas time (*silent night*), mistletoe and wine, (*holy night!*)
Children singing (D) Christian rhyme.
With logs on the fire and gifts on the tree,
A time to (D7) rejoice in the (G) good that we see.

(G) Christmas time, (*Christmas time*) mistletoe and wine,
Children singing (D) Christian rhyme.
With logs on the fire and gifts on the tree,
A time to (D7) rejoice in the (G) good that we see.

G

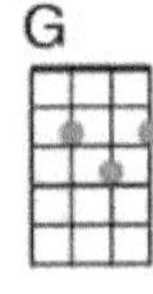

Em

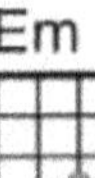

D

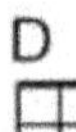

C

A

D7

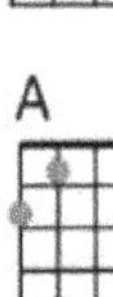

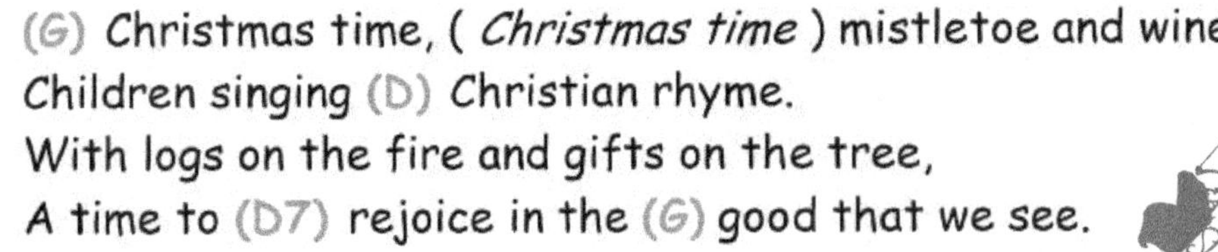

<u>O Come All Ye Faithful</u> —Wade & Oakeley

 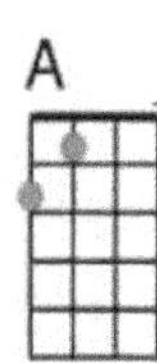 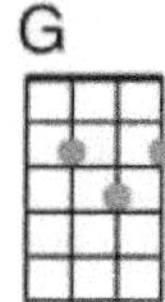 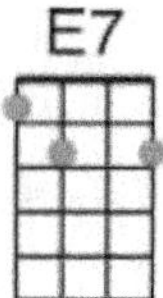

O (D) come all ye (A) faithful, (D) joyful and (A) triumphant,
O (G) come ye, o (A) come ye to Be - (E7) -eth (A) -lehem.
(D) Come and be (G) hold him, (A) born the (G) King of (A) Angels.

(D) Oh come, let us adore him,
Oh come, let us adore him,
O (G) come, let us a-(A)-dore (D)-hi-(G)-im ,
(D) Christ (A) the (D) Lord.

(D) Sing choirs of (A) angels (D) sing in exul-(A)-tation
(G) Sing all ye (A) citizens of he-(E7)-aven (A) above.
(D) Glory to (G) God (A) in (G) the (A) highest.

(D) Oh come, let us adore him, (*Oh come!*)
Oh come, let us adore him,   (*Oh come!*)
O (G) come, let us a-(A)-dore (D)-hi-(G)-im ,
(D) Christ (A) the (D) Lord.

Rockin' Around the Christmas Tree
—John Marks

(G) Rocking around the Christmas tree
At the (D) Christmas party hop.
Mistletoe hung where you can see
Every couple try to (G) stop.
Rocking around the Christmas tree
Let the (D) Christmas spirit ring
Later we'll have some pumpkin pie
And we'll do some carol-(G)-ling.

(C) You will get a sentimental (Bm) feeling when you hear
(C) Voices singing, ' Let's be jolly,
(A) Deck the halls with (D) boughs of holly'.
(G) Rocking around the Christmas tree
Have a (D) happy holiday.
Everyone dancing merrily
In the new old-fashioned (G) way.

(C) You will get a sentimental (Bm) feeling when you hear
(C) Voices singing, ' Let's be jolly,
(A) Deck the halls with (D) boughs of holly'.
((A) *Fa la la la* (D) *laaa, la la* (A) *la* (D) *laa*)

(G) Rocking around the Christmas tree
Let the (D) Christmas spirit ring
Later we'll have some pumpkin pie
And we'll do some carol-(G)-ling.
Rocking around the Christmas tree
Have a (D) happy holiday.
Everyone dancing merrily in the
New - Old - Fashioned (G) Way. (D) (G)

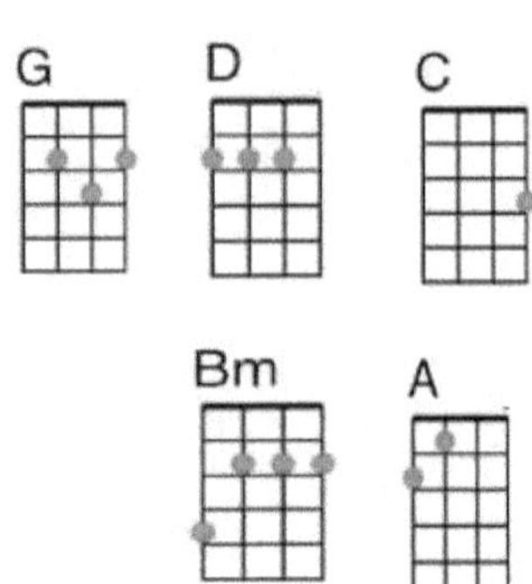

<u>Rudolf The Red Nosed Reindeer —</u>
John Marks

  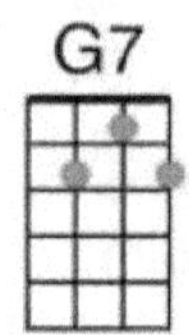 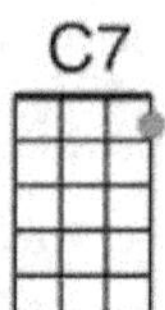 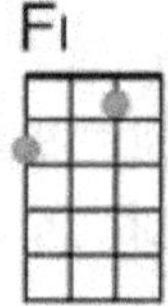 

(C) Rudolph, the red-nosed reindeer
Had a very shiny (G) nose,
And if you ever saw it,
 (G7) You would even say it (C) glows.
All of the other reindeer
Used to laugh and call him (G) names
They never let poor Rudolph
(G7) Join in any reindeer (C) games. (C7)

(F) Then one foggy (C) Christmas Eve
(G) Santa came to (C) say,
(G) "Rudolph with your (E7) nose so bright,
(D) Won't you guide my (G7) sleigh tonight?"
(C) Then all the reindeer loved him
And they shouted out with (G) glee,
"Rudolph the red-nosed reindeer,
(G7) You'll go down in (C) history! "

<u>Santa Claus Is Comin' To Town—</u>
Gillespie & Coots

You (C) better watch out, you (F) better not cry,
You (C) better not pout, I'm (F) telling you why.
(C) Santa Claus is (F) coming to town
(C) Santa Claus is (F) coming to town
(C) Santa (Am) Claus is (F) coming (G) to town (C) (G)

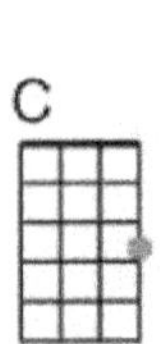

He's (C) making a list, he's (F) checking it twice,
He's (C) gonna find out who's (F) naughty or nice.
(C) Santa Claus is (F) coming to town
(C) Santa Claus is (F) coming to town
(C) Santa (Am) Claus is (F) coming (G) to town (C)

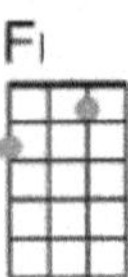

He sees you when you're (F) sleeping,
He (C) knows when you're (F) awake,
He (D) knows if you've been (G) bad or good
So be (D) good for goodness (G) sake,

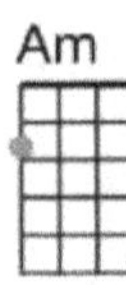

Oh, you (C) better watch out, you (F) better not cry,
You (C) better not pout, I'm (F) telling you why.
(C) Santa Claus is (F) coming to town
(C) Santa Claus is (F) coming to town
(C) Santa (Am) Claus is (F) coming (G) to town (C)

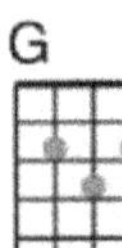

He sees you when you're (F) sleeping,
He (C) knows when you're (F) awake,
He (D) knows if you've been (G) bad or good
So be (D) good for goodness (G) sake,

Oh, you (C) better watch out, you (F) better not cry,
You (C) better not pout, I'm (F) telling you why.
(C) Santa Claus is (F) coming to town
(C) Santa Claus is (F) coming to town
(*Half time*)
(C) Santa   (Am) Claus is   (F) coming (G) to town (C)

Silent Night—
Mohr & Gruber

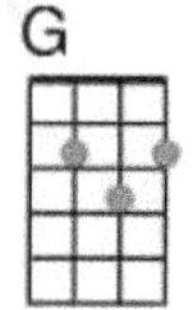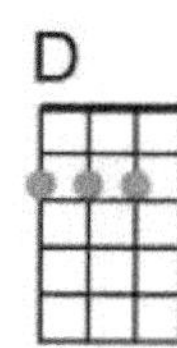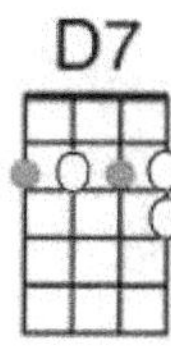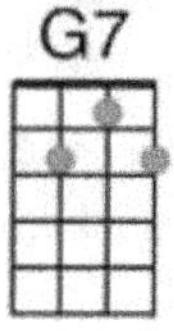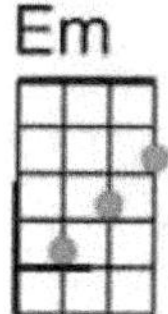

(G) Silent night, holy night!
(D) All is (D7) calm, (G) all is (G7) bright,
(C) Round yon virgin, (G) mother and (G7) child,
(C) Holy infant so (G) tender and mild,
(D) Sleep in (D7) heavenly (G) peace (Em)
(G) Sleep in (D7) heavenly (G) peace. (C)(G)

Silent night, holy night!
(D) Shepherds (D7) quake (G) at the (G7) sight
(C) Glories stream from (G) heaven (G7) afar
(C) Heavenly hosts sing (G) alleluia
(D) Christ the (D7) saviour is (G) born (Em)
(G) Christ the (D7) saviour is (G) born. (C)(G)

Silent night, holy night!
(D) Son of (D7) God, (G) love's pure (G7) light
(C) Radiant beams from (G) thy holy (G7) face,
(C) With the dawn of (G) redeeming grace
(D) Jesus (D7) Lord at thy (G) birth (Em)
(G) Jesus (D7) Lord at thy (G) birth.

<u>Stop The Cavalry</u> —Jona Lewie

(A) Hey Mister Churchill (E7) comes over here
(A) To say we're doing (E7) splendidly,
(A) But it's very cold (E7) out here in the snow
(A) Marching to and from the (E7) enemy.
(A) Oh I say it's tough, (E7) I have had enough
(A) Can you stop the (E7) cavalry? (A)

Da da da da da, (E7) da da da da da,
(A) da da da da da, (E7) da da daaa
(A) Da da da da da, (E7) da da da da da
(A) Da da da da (E7) daa da (A) daaa

(A) I have had to fight (E7) almost every night
(A) Down throughout the (E7) centuries,
(A) That is when I say (E7) oh yes, yet again,
(A) Can you stop the (E7) cavalry? (A)

(E7) Mary proudly (A) waits at home
(E7) In the nuclear (A) fallout zone
(E7) Wish I could be (A) dancing now,
(E7) In the arms of the (A) girl I love.

(E7) Du bu du bu dum dum, du bu du bu dum
Du bu (A) dum dum du bu dum du bu du bu dum
(E7) Du bu du bu dum dum, du bu du bu dum
Du bu (A) dum dum du bu dum du bu du bu dum
(G) Wish I was at home for (D) Christmas...
(A)(D)(A)(D)(A)(D)(A)
(E7) Wish I could be (A) dancing now,
(E7) In the arms of the (A) girl I love.
(E7) Mary proudly (A) waits at home
(E7) She's been waiting (A) two years long

(E7) Du bu du bu dum dum, du bu du bu dum
Du bu (A) dum dum du bu dum du bu du bu dum
(E7) Du bu du bu dum dum, du bu du bu dum
Du bu (A) dum dum du bu dum du bu du bu dum
(G) Wish I was at home for (D) Christmas...
(A)(D)(A)(D) (E7) (A)

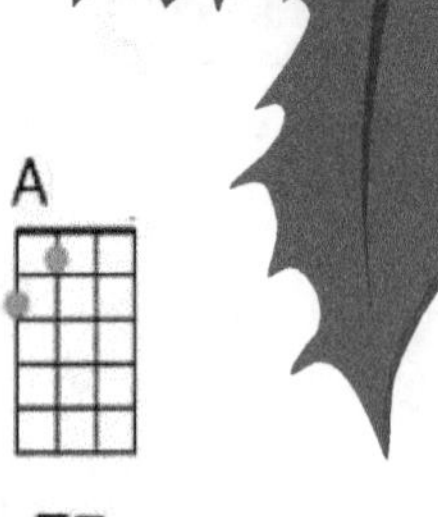
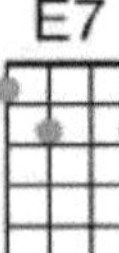
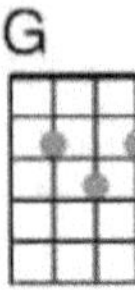
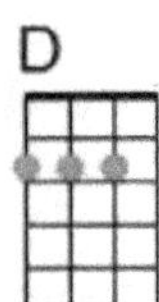

The Twelve Days of Christmas— Traditional

On the (C) **first** day of Christmas my (G) true love gave to (C) me :
A partridge in a (G) pear (C) tree.

On the (C) **second** day of Christmas my (G) true love gave to (C) me :
(G) Two turtle-doves and a (C) partridge in a (G) pear (C) tree.

On the (C) **third** day of Christmas my (G) true love gave to (C) me :
(G) Three French hens, two turtle-doves and a
(C) Partridge in a (G) pear (C) tree.

On the (C) **fourth** day of Christmas my (G) true love gave to (C) me :
(G) Four calling birds, three French hens, two turtle-doves and a
(C) Partridge in a (G) pear (C) tree.

On the (C) **fifth** day of Christmas my (G) true love gave to (C) me :
➤ (Em) Five (D) golden (G) rings... (G7)
(C) Four calling birds, (F) three French hens, (G) two turtle-doves
And a (C) partridge in a (G) pear (C) tree.

On the (C) **sixth** day of Christmas my (G) true love gave to (C) me :
(G) Six geese-a-laying... ..... (*Repeat from arrow*)

On the (C) **seventh** day of Christmas my (G) true love gave to (C) me :
(G) Seven swans-a-swimming, six geese-a-laying... (*Repeat from arrow*)

On the (C) **eighth** day of Christmas my (G) true love gave to (C) me :
(G) Eight maids-a-milking,
Seven swans-a-swimming, six geese-a-laying... (*Repeat from arrow*)

On the (C) **ninth** day of Christmas my (G) true love gave to (C) me :
(G) Nine ladies dancing, eight maids-a-milking,
Seven swans-a-swimming, six geese-a-laying... (*Repeat from arrow*)

On the (C) **tenth** day of Christmas my (G) true love gave to (C) me :
(G) Ten Lords-a-leaping, nine ladies dancing, eight maids-a-milking,
Seven swans-a-swimming, six geese-a-laying... (*Repeat from arrow*)

On the (C) **eleventh** day of Christmas my (G) true love gave to (C) me :
(G) Eleven pipers piping, ten Lords-a-leaping, nine ladies dancing, eight maids-a-
milking, seven swans-a-swimming, six geese-a-laying... (*Repeat from arrow*)

On the (C) **twelfth** day of Christmas my (G) true love gave to (C) me :
(G) Twelve drummers drumming, eleven pipers piping, ten Lords-a-leaping, nine
ladies dancing, eight maids-a-milking, seven swans-a-swimming, six geese-a-
laying... (*Repeat from arrow*)

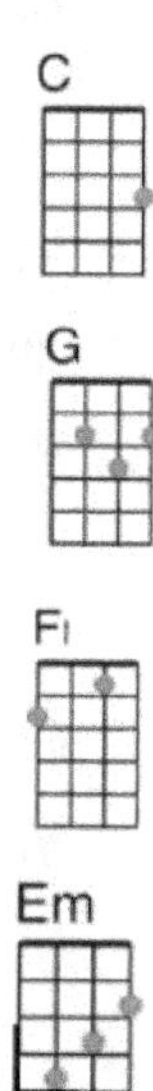

C

G

F

Em

G7

<u>We Wish You A Merry Christmas—</u>
Traditional

We (G) wish you a merry (C) Christmas,
We (A) wish you a merry (D) Christmas,
We (B) wish you a merry (Em) Christmas and a
(C) Happy (D) new (G) year.

Good tidings we (D) bring to (Em) you and your (D) kin,
We (G) wish you a merry (D) Christmas and a
(C) Happy (D) new (G) year.

Oh (G) bring us some figgy (C) pudding,
Oh (A) bring us some figgy (D) pudding,
Oh (B) bring us some figgy (Em) pudding,
And (C) bring it (D) out (G) here!

Good tidings we (D) bring to (Em) you and your (D) kin,
We (G) wish you a merry (D) Christmas and a
(C) Happy (D) new (G) year.

We (G) won't go until we (C) get some,
We (A) won't go until we (D) get some,
We (B) won't go until we (Em) get some,
So (C) bring some (D) out (G) here!

Good tidings we (D) bring to (Em) you and your (D) kin,
We (G) wish you a merry (D) Christmas and a
(C) Happy (D) new (G) year.

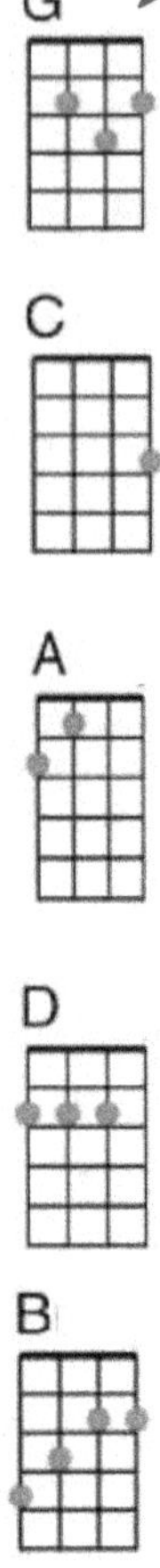

When A Child Is Born—Zacar & Jay

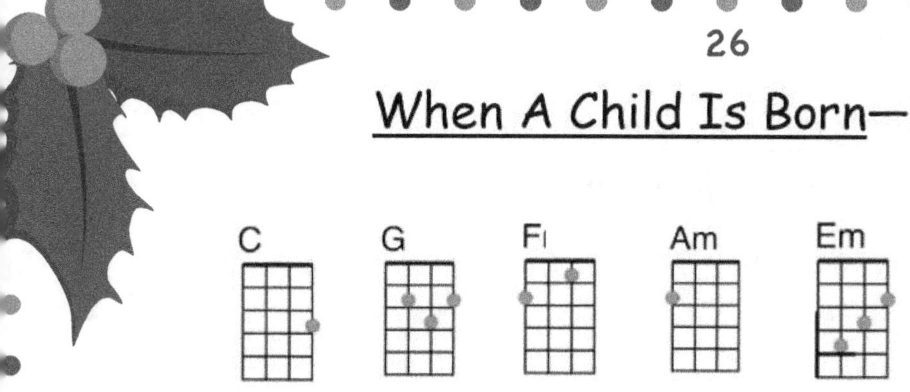

A ray of (C) hope (G) flickers in the (C) sky, (F)(C)
A tiny star (Am) lights up way up (G) high, (F)(G)
All (F) across the land (G) dawns a brand new (Em) morn ,
(Am) This comes to (G) pass when a (Dm) child is (C) born.

A silent (C) wish (G) sails the seven (C) seas, (F)(C)
The winds of change (Am) whisper in the (G) trees (F)(G)
All the (F) walls of doubt (G) crumble tossed and (Em) torn ,
(Am) This comes to (G) pass when a (Dm) child is (C) born.

A rosy (C) dawn (G) settles all (C) around, (F)(C)
You get the feel (Am) you're on solid (G) ground (F)(G)
For a (F) spell or two (G) no-one seems (Em) forlorn ,
(Am) This comes to (G) pass when a (Dm) child is (C) born.

It's all a (C) dream, (G) an illusion (C) now, (F)(C)
It must come true (Am) sometime soon (G) somehow. (F)(G)
All (F) across the land (G) dawns a brand new (Em) morn ,
(Am) This comes to (G) pass when a (Dm) child is (C) born. (F)(C)

Winter Wonderland—
Smith & Bernard

Sleigh bells (G) ring, are you listenin'?
In the (D) lane, snow is glistening.
A (D7) beautiful (Am) sight, we're (D) happy (Am) tonight,
(A) Walking in a (D) winter (G) wonderland.

Gone (G) away is the blue bird
Here to (D) stay is the new bird
He (D7) sings a love (Am) song as (D) we go (Am) along,
(A) Walking in a (D) winter (G) wonderland.

(B) In the meadow (F#) we can build a (B) snowman,
Then pretend that (F#) he is Parson (B) Brown.
(D) He'll say, "Are you (A) married ?" We'll say, (D) "No man,
But you can (A) do the job when you're in (D) town." (D7)

Later (G) on we'll conspire
As we (D) dream by the fire,
To (D7) face un-(Am)-afraid the (D) plans that we (Am) made,
(A) Walking in a (D) winter (G) wonderland.

(B) In the meadow (F#) we can build a (B) snowman,
Then pretend that (F#) he's a circus (B) clown.
(D) We'll have lots of (A) fun with mister (D) snowman
Until the (A) other kiddies knock him (D) down. (D7)

Later (G) on we'll conspire
As we (D) dream by the fire,
To (D7) face un-(Am)-afraid the (D) plans that we (Am) made,
(A) Walking in a (D) winter (G) wonderland. (G7)
(A) Walking, (D7) walking in a winter wonder-(G)-land. (D) (G)